CALIFORNIA A TO Z

by
DOROTHY
HINES WEAVER

Illustrated by
KAY
WACKER

The illustrations were done in dyes and color pencils on illustration board
The text type was set in Stempel Garamond
The display type was set in Shaka Zulu
Composed in the United States of America
Designed by Jennifer Schaber
Production Supervised by Lisa Brownfield

Printed in Hong Kong by Wing King Tong Company Limited

First Impression
ISBN 0-87358-682-4

Library of Congress Catalog Card Number pending

0646/7.5M/4-99

In celebration of the miracle birth of our baby Kelci and to her cousin, Jacob. With thanks to Kay's husband, Tim, for his support.

Amusement parks attracting all ages

Aa

Boaters breezing by Bodega Bay

Bb

Cable cars clanging in Chinatown

Cc

Dolphins dip and dive by Dana Point

Dd

Egret encircling an estuary

Ee

Fortress founded on the frontier

Grizzlies growled in the Golden State

G g

Historic homes highlighted in Heritage Park

Hh

Irrigation invigorating the Imperial Valley

Jellyfish jiggling by a jetty

Kinglets keep moving in Kings Canyon

Kk

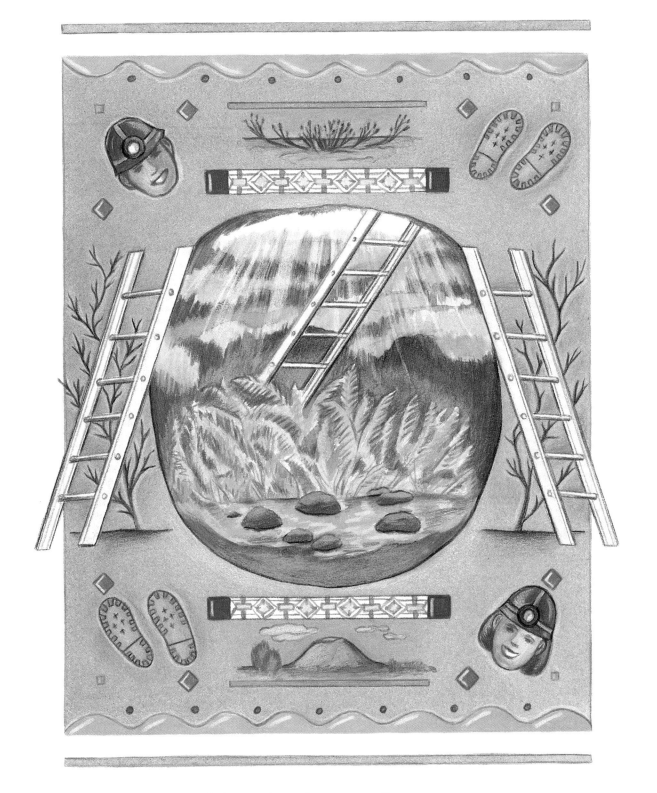

Ladders leading to lava caves

L l

Monarchs migrating to Monterey

Mm

Nautical museum nestled in Newport

Nn

Otters observed by oceanographers

Poppies prospering by the Pacific

Pp

Quail plant quivering during a quake

Qq

Raccoon roaming the redwood forest

Rr

Stars shining on studio stages

Ss

Tortoise trekking towards Twentynine Palms

Tt

Urchin unhurried underwater

Uu

Vineyards viewed in the valleys

Whale watching at the waterfront

X-ray fish in an exotic exhibit

Xx

Yellowthroat yodeling in Yosemite

Yy

Zebraperch zipping by Zuma Beach

Zz

California became our thirty-first state on September 9, 1850. Spanish explorers named California after a fabled island paradise in a sixteenth-century novel. The state colors are blue and gold. In 1911 the bear flag was adopted as the state's official flag. The state motto is Eureka. It appears at the top of the state seal and is Greek for "I have found it."

amusement parks California is known for its many theme park attractions that provide exciting family entertainment. They include Disneyland, Knott's Berry Farm, Sea World, Six Flags California, Marine World, and Universal Studios.

Bodega Bay This historic north coast fishing community was discovered by the Spanish in 1775. It was established as a port by Russian settlers. A Fisherman's Festival with a colorful boat parade is held annually.

cable cars These vehicles can climb the steep hills of spectacular San Francisco. They are pulled along by moving steel cables under the street. The National Park Service declared the cable car a National Historic Landmark in 1964.

Chinatown San Francisco's Chinatown is the largest Chinese community outside Asia. It was settled in the 1800s. Chinatown, with its interesting shops and fine restaurants, is a major northern California attraction.

Dana Point This picturesque area is on the coast south of Laguna Beach. It is named for Richard Henry Dana who wrote *Two Years Before the Mast*. The Orange County Marine Institute offers tours aboard a replica of his brig, *The Pilgrim*.

dolphins Common dolphins are graceful mammals that dwell in deep waters near the coast. They can leap above the water and they often travel in large groups.

egret The snowy egret is a medium-sized heron that likes marshy areas near lakes or estuaries. It sometimes makes platform nests on willows or in bushes.

estuary An estuary is an inlet, sound, or bay where fresh water and tidal water meet. It supports a variety of marine life. Estuaries are found on the west coast.

fortress Sutter's Fort State Historic Park is located in midtown Sacramento. It was built originally in 1840 by California pioneer John Sutter. In 1848 gold was discovered at Sutter's mill. Sutter's settlement was the beginning of Sacramento, which became the state capital in 1854.

frontier This area was the border between early western settlements and undeveloped territories.

golden state California's nickname is "The Golden State" because of its sunshine and the Gold Rush–era.

grizzlies The grizzly bear is the state animal of California. At one time grizzlies roamed the mountains and meadows but they became extinct in California in the 1920s. The grizzly bear is displayed on the state flag.

Heritage Park This lovely county park preserves examples of Victorian architecture. It is located in San Diego's historic Old Town. San Diego is the oldest city in California and was founded by Father Junipero Serra in 1769.

Imperial Valley Irrigation has turned this desert land into a fertile agricultural region. It is in the southern part of the state.

jellyfish These sea invertebrates have soft, quivering bodies and tentacles with stinging cells. There are many kinds of jellyfish and they come in different sizes and colors.

jetty A jetty is a kind of wall extending out into the water to protect a pier or harbor from current.

kinglets The ruby-crowned kinglet is small and very active. It seems to flick its wings continually and make quick movements. In the summer it can be found in the forest areas of Kings Canyon and then flying to the foothills for the winter.

Kings Canyon Sequoia and Kings Canyon National Parks are in the east central part of the state in the Sierra Nevada Mountains. Groves of giant sequoias, the largest trees on earth, thrive within the parks. Mount Whitney, the state's highest peak, is on the eastern edge of this area.

lava caves There are over three hundred caves within Lava Beds National Monument in northeastern California. Lava tube caves are a result of volcanic activity. Ladders have been installed in some of these fascinating caves to make access easier.

monarchs Monarch butterflies migrate in large numbers to the Monterey Peninsula. Every year they return to Pacific Grove, which is called "Butterfly City USA."

Monterey The scenic Monterey Peninsula is on the central coast. The Lone Cypress is well known in this area. The historic city of Monterey was the capital when Mexico and Spain ruled California. Mission San Carlos Borromeo del Rio Carmelo is nearby on the peninsula in charming Carmel.

nautical museum The Newport Harbor Nautical Museum is located in Newport Beach on a riverboat replica, the *Pride of Newport.* It preserves the region's heritage with maritime displays and boat exhibits.

Newport The Newport yacht harbor is one of the largest and busiest in the world. Newport Beach is a colorful resort city located on the coast south of Los Angeles.

oceanographers These scientists study all aspects of the ocean.

otters Sea otters are playful mammals with webbed feet. They live close to shore, mainly along the central coast. They sleep in kelp beds and feed while floating on their backs. They use rocks to crack open shells.

poppies The golden poppy, the state flower, thrives along the Pacific coast. It colors hillsides and valleys. Its petals open in full sunshine and close at night and on foggy days.

quail plant This leafy plant is a creeper with coiled flowers. It is named for the bird that eats its fruit. The California valley quail is the state bird.

quake Earthquakes are sometimes felt in the state. The ground suddenly trembles due to fault lines below the earth's surface.

raccoon This small nocturnal animal can climb trees and often sleeps in hollow trees. Most nights are spent searching for food.

redwood forest The California redwood is the state tree. Redwood National and State Parks are located along the scenic northwest coast. They preserve groves of ancient redwoods including the world's tallest trees.

stars Many celebrities perform in Los Angeles. Hollywood is known throughout the world for its movie and television industries. Attractions include studio tours and the Walk of Fame.

tortoise The desert tortoise is the state reptile. It travels slowly in desert regions and protects itself by withdrawing into its shell. It can go for long periods without water. During the winter it digs burrows or dens for hibernation.

Twentynine Palms This Mojave desert community is the northern gateway to Joshua Tree National Monument. Stands of Joshua trees are found in this vast parkland where the high Mojave meets the lower Colorado desert.

urchin The red sea urchin is found on rocky shores and in off-shore waters. It travels slowly using its movable sharp spines or tiny tube feet.

vineyards Grapes are cultivated in the inland valleys of Napa and Sonoma in the northern part of the state. Hot air-ballooning affords an excellent view of some of these well-known valley vineyards.

waterfront Some excellent places to view the whales from shore include Point Loma at Cabrillo National Monument in San Diego, Point Lobos and Big Sur in Monterey County, Davenport Landing in Santa Cruz County, and Point Reyes National Seashore in Marin County.

whale The California gray whale is the state marine mammal. This aquatic giant is seen along the Pacific coast during its fall migration to Baja California and again in the spring when it returns to the Arctic.

x-ray fish This unique fish with its transparent body is an aquarium favorite. Outstanding California aquariums include the Monterey Bay Aquarium, Stephen Birch Aquarium-Museum at Scripps Institute of Oceanography in La Jolla, and the Steinhart Aquarium in San Francisco.

yellowthroat The common yellowthroat is a wren-like warbler. The male's repeated song is loud and high-pitched. The female's nest is cup-shaped and usually is in grass or shrubs near the ground.

Yosemite This beautiful national park is in east central California. It is known for its groves of giant sequoias, granite cliffs and domes, high cascading waterfalls, alpine wilderness, and the spectacular Yosemite Valley.

zebraperch Striped zebraperch often swim in shallow inshore areas. They can be found along the coast from the Gulf of California to Monterey Bay.

Zuma Beach This popular public beach is on the Malibu coast. It is a favorite place for surfing.

DOROTHY HINES WEAVER and KAY WACKER, the mother-daughter team that wrote and illustrated Rising Moon's *Arizona A to Z* and *New Mexico A to Z,* lived in northern California for five years and spent a lot of time in southern California where Dorothy's parents lived. They have now lived in Arizona for more than twenty years.

DOROTHY received her B.S. in Education from the University of Nebraska at Omaha and is a former elementary teacher and school librarian. She has three daughters and six grandchildren.

KAY received her B.F.A. with an emphasis in illustration from Northern Arizona University and has worked as an illustrator for the past eleven years. Kay has three children, ages nine, two, and one.

David Slough